Everyday Banking

Consumer Banking

ERNESTINE GIESECKE

Heinemann Library
Chicago, Illinois

© 2003 Reed Educational & Professional Publishing
Published by Heinemann Library,
an imprint of Reed Educational & Professional Publishing,
Chicago, Illinois

Customer Service 888-454-2279
Visit our website at www.heinemannlibrary.com

Designed by Herman Adler Design
Printed and bound in the United States by Lake Book
Manufacturing, Inc.

07 06 05 04 03
10 9 8 7 6 5 4 3 2 1

Library of Congress Cataloging-in-Publication Data
Giesecke, Ernestine, 1945-
  Everyday banking : consumer banking / Ernestine Giesecke.
    v. cm. — (Everyday economics)
Includes bibliographical references and index.
Contents: Earning money — Spending money — Saving
money — Earning interest — Saving accounts — Checking
accounts — Reconciling an account — Processing checks —
Paying without checks — Charge cards — Credit cards —
Credit card cost — Debit and smart cards — ATM cards —
Loans — Long-term loans — Short-term loans — Credit —
Credit reports — Fixing credit problems — Open a savings
account.
  ISBN 1-58810-489-3 (HC), 1-58810-952-6 (Pbk.)
  1. Children—Finance, Personal—Juvenile literature.
2. Banks and banking—Juvenile literature. 3. Finance,
Personal—Juvenile literature. [1. Finance, Personal. 2. Banks
and banking.] I. Title.
  HG179 .G482 2002
  332.1'7—dc21
                              2002000802

Acknowledgments
The author and publisher are grateful to the following for
permission to reproduce copyright material:
Cover photograph by Keith Brofsky/PhotoDisc
pp. 2, 5BR, 31, 33 PhotoDisc; pp. 5TR, 6R, 9B, 12R, 24, 40
David Young-Wolff/PhotoEdit, Inc.; pp. 5TL, 7, 9T, 15 Tony
Freeman/PhotoEdit, Inc.; p. 5B Mark Richards/PhotoEdit,
Inc.; p. 6L Elena Rooraid/PhotoEdit, Inc.; pp. 8, 12L, 17, 22,
43 Michael Brosilow/Heinemann Library; pp. 13, 32 Jeff
Greenberg/Visuals Unlimited; pp. 14, 18 Bill
Aron/PhotoEdit, Inc.; p. 20 Reuters New Media Inc./Corbis;
p. 21 Culver Pictures; p. 23B Tom McCarthy/PhotoEdit,
Inc.; pp. 23T, 30 Spencer Grant/PhotoEdit, Inc.; p. 34 Dana
White/PhotoEdit, Inc.; p. 38 Arthur Hill/Visuals Unlimited

Every effort has been made to contact copyright holders of
any material reproduced in this book. Any omissions will be
rectified in subsequent printings if notice is given to the
publisher.

Note to the Reader: Some words are shown in
bold, **like this.** You can find out what they mean
by looking in the glossary.

Contents

Earning Money

Money is a method of exchange—it can be given in exchange for things people want and need. Money gives people a way to purchase **goods,** such as clothes, food, and computers; and **services,** such as street cleaning, hospital care, and hairstyling. Businesses and individuals accept money as payment for goods and services. Governments accept money for payment of taxes and **debts.**

Before people can spend anything, they have to get money, usually by earning it. When people work, they receive money. The money people earn is called their **income.** Some people earn income by running their own businesses. They may sell goods such as make-up or provide a service such as hairstyling. An allowance is a form of income that is usually for young people. They may earn an allowance by doing chores around the house or looking after their younger siblings.

Other people earn income in the form of **wages.** Wages are income based on the number of hours a worker works or the number of items she or he produces. For example, a cashier at a fast-food restaurant may earn $6.50 for each hour he or she works. A farm worker may earn $0.80 for each crate of eggs he or she gathers.

A **salary** is another form of income. A person's salary is income that remains the same for a fixed period of time, such as a year. For example, an accountant at a company may earn a salary of $25,000 a year.

Some kinds of income, such as gifts, **grants,** and unemployment **benefits,** are called **unearned income.** No goods or services are involved in unearned income.

People can earn money in a variety of ways.

Spending Money

Money offers people a way to make choices. People may choose to use their **income** to take care of their needs. That is, they may spend their income on **goods** such as food, clothing, housing, or medicine that they need to survive. On the other hand, people may choose to use their income on things they want but could survive without. For example, they may buy magazines, CDs, or video games.

Suppose you choose to buy a new pair of shoes or a puzzle to share with your family. Either way, you will have made a choice about what to do with your money. Once you spend the money for the shoes or puzzle, you no longer have it to use for anything else.

People often spend their money on things they need. They may also spend money on things they want.

Money spent at a pharmacy circulates through the **economy.** Some of it goes to pay the pharmacist for his work. Some pays for the chemicals to make the medicine, as well as for research to invent new medicines.

However, the money does not disappear. Some of it pays the **wages** of the store clerks. Some money goes to the companies who made the shoes and the puzzle. The shoe company and the puzzle company use the money to pay the workers who made the shoes and the puzzle. The companies will also buy supplies to make more shoes and produce more puzzles. The money you spend in one place can end up in many different faraway places, in the hands of many different people.

Saving Money

Many people save part of their **income**. They may be saving for a special purchase, such as a bicycle or vacation trip. People also save money toward long-term goals such as paying for college tuition or buying a home. Many individuals save money for a "rainy day," too. This money is available for an emergency or an unplanned purchase.

Some people hide the money they save in a drawer or shoebox. But this money is easy to get to, and it could be lost or stolen. A more effective idea is to **deposit** it in a bank or other **financial institution**. Banks safeguard, or keep safe, all the money that people deposit. They keep cash available for people to **withdraw** when they need it, and they have insurance to cover any losses from robberies.

Know It

Savings banks, savings and loan associations, and credit unions are often called "thrifts" because their goal is to encourage saving.

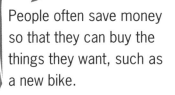

People often save money so that they can buy the things they want, such as a new bike.

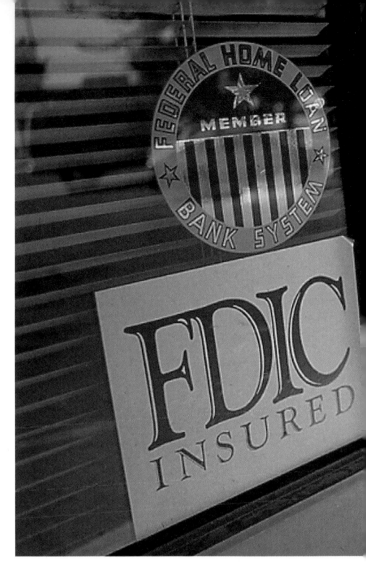

More importantly, government agencies insure the money that people deposit in banks. The **Federal** Deposit Insurance Corporation (FDIC) insures deposits in nearly all the country's banks. The Savings Association Insurance Fund (SAIF) insures deposits in savings and loan institutions, and the National Credit Union Share Insurance Fund insures accounts at credit unions. Each of these agencies insures savings accounts up to a maximum deposit of $100,000.

Earning Interest

Depositing money in a bank savings account offers **benefits.** For one thing, it is not as easy to spend as money kept at the bank. Not only does the bank keep the money safe, but it also pays the customer for depositing the money. The money a bank pays customers for their deposits is called **interest.** Interest is usually paid as a percent of the total amount deposited. The percent paid is called the interest rate.

The amount of interest an account earns mainly depends on four things: how much money is in the account, how long the money is left in the account, how high the interest rate is, and what type of interest is applied to the account. Suppose Ace Bank offers an **annual** rate of five percent interest on a savings account. There is $100 in the account, and the money is left in the account for a year. If the interest is figured out at the end of the year, the account will earn $5 in interest. An account with more money would earn more interest.

Know It

The word percent means "for each one hundred." If a savings account earns three percent interest, it will earn $3 for every $100 in the account. This is the same as earning three cents for every dollar in the account.

There are two types of interest, simple interest and compound interest. If an account earns simple interest, the interest rate is applied only to the original amount deposited. This is true no matter how large the account **balance** grows. On the other hand, if an account earns compound interest, the interest rate is applied to the original deposit amount plus any interest already earned. Savings that earn compound interest grow faster than savings that earn simple interest, because each time the amount of interest is based on a larger total. Compound interest accounts can earn money even faster when the interest is compounded more often—for example, every three months instead of once a year.

If an account earns simple interest, the interest rate applies only to the original deposit amount. A deposit of $100 will earn $25 in five years.

Simple Interest

Length of time deposit is held	Starting amount	Interest (Interest rate of five percent per year)	Ending amount
1 year	$ 100.00	$ 5.00	$ 105.00
2 years	$ 105.00	$ 5.00	$ 110.00
3 years	$ 110.00	$ 5.00	$ 115.00
4 years	$ 115.00	$ 5.00	$ 120.00
5 years	$ 120.00	$ 5.00	$ 125.00

In compound interest, the interest rate is applied to the original deposit plus any interest already earned. If $100 earns five percent interest compounded quarterly—four times a year—the total interest earned after five years is $28.20.

Compound Interest

Length of time deposit is held	Starting amount	Interest (Interest rate of five percent per year)	Ending amount
3 months	$ 100.00	$ 1.25	$ 101.25
6 months	$ 101.25	$ 1.27	$ 102.52
9 months	$ 102.52	$ 1.28	$ 103.80
12 months	$ 103.80	$ 1.30	$ 105.10
4 years, 9 months	$ 125.03	$ 1.59	$ 126.62
5 years	$ 126.62	$ 1.58	$ 128.20

Saving Accounts

One of the most common forms of savings is the passbook savings account. A passbook is a book where you can record every **deposit, interest** payment, and **withdrawal.** A passbook savings account usually earns a low rate called **minimum** interest. The customer can withdraw any or all of his or her deposit without giving the bank advance notice.

This passbook shows the date and amount of every savings deposit. It also shows how much interest the deposits have earned.

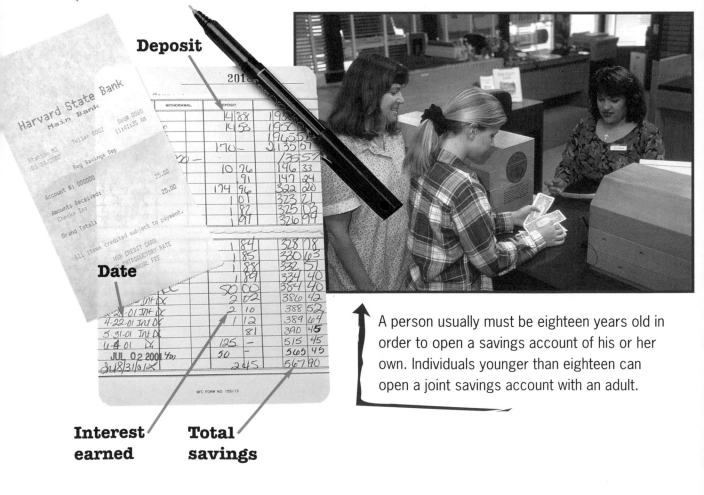

A person usually must be eighteen years old in order to open a savings account of his or her own. Individuals younger than eighteen can open a joint savings account with an adult.

Deposit

Date

Interest earned

Total savings

Some banks offer a form of deposit called a time deposit. These savings accounts that are held for a fixed length of time are known as certificates of deposit, or CDs. A CD usually earns higher interest than a passbook savings account. Also, CDs held for a longer time earn higher interest rates than do shorter-term CDs. However, there is a **penalty** for withdrawing the deposit before the end of the fixed time period. CDs are often available for terms such as three months, six months, one year, or three years.

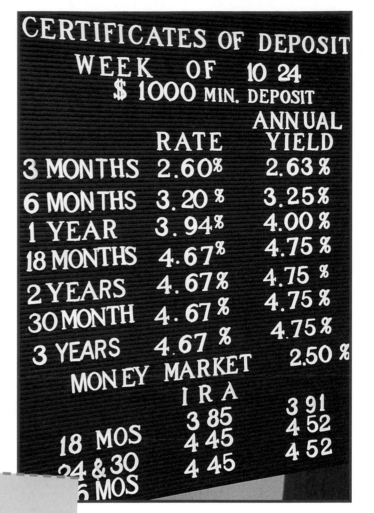

This bank pays 2.60 percent interest for a three month CD. The interest is compounded quarterly, or four times a year, and is equal to a once-a-year rate (**annual** percentage yield) of 2.63 percent.

Dutch deposits

Some of the earliest deposits made to a bank were not savings, strictly speaking. The Bank of Amsterdam, established in 1609, accepted deposits of gold and silver from **merchants.** The bank charged a fee for keeping the valuable metals safe and gave merchants receipts for their valuables. Keeping the gold and silver on deposit with the bank allowed merchants to pay for goods without actually moving the gold or silver from one place to another. Instead, merchants simply traded the receipts given to them by the bank.

Checking Accounts

Today, many people do not use cash when they pay for purchases at the grocery store, music store, or dentist's office. Instead of cash, these people pay with personal checks. A check is a written instruction to a specific bank telling it to pay a certain amount of money to a particular individual or business. The check gives the bank permission to take that amount of money out of the customer's checking account and to send it to the person or business whose name is written on the check.

An individual must keep track of the checks he or she has written to know how much money is in a checking account. Each **transaction**

Writing a check is one way to make a purchase without using actual cash. It is important to record the amount of the check in the check register.

Writing a check for which there are not sufficient funds is expensive. First, the store receiving the check may charge a returned check fee of $15 to $30. The bank itself charges a similar fee. Some banks will even close an account if there are more than three returned checks in a year.

should be recorded in a small booklet called a check register. Every time the customer writes a check, he or she should subtract the amount of the check from the **balance** of the account. Any **deposits** made to the account should be added to the balance. The customer is responsible for making certain that the account has enough money to pay every check.

Sometimes a check cannot be paid because the account does not have enough money in it. Checks like these are returned to the person who wrote them. The check will be marked NSF, meaning "not sufficient **funds.**" The bank charges a fee for handling a returned check, usually from $20 to $30. It is against the law to knowingly write a check that your account does not have enough money to pay.

Know It

Because NSF checks are "bounced back" to the check writer, they are sometimes called "rubber checks" or "bounced checks."

Balancing an Account

Once a month, the bank sends a statement to each checking account customer. The statement lists all the checks and **deposits** the bank recorded for the customer's account. The customer should compare his or her own account records with the bank's records. This is called balancing the account.

Statements from different banks may look different from one another. However, all statements contain the same kinds of information. Statements list the name on the account, the account number, the date of the statement, and the beginning and ending date for the statement.

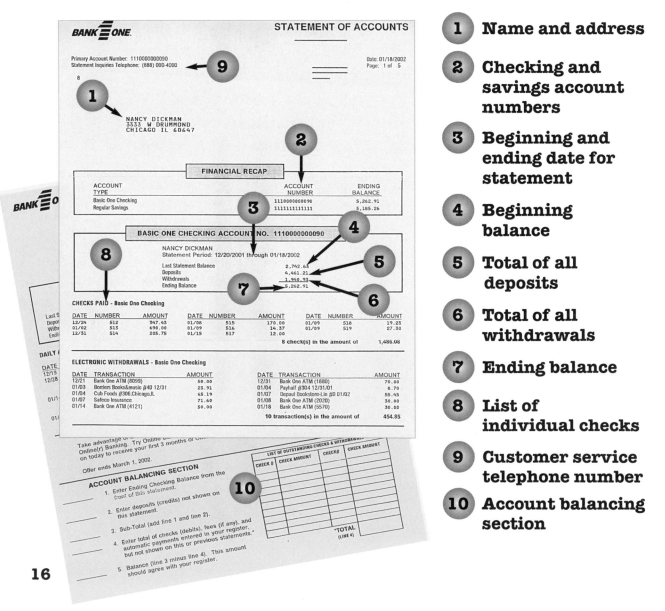

1. **Name and address**

2. **Checking and savings account numbers**

3. **Beginning and ending date for statement**

4. **Beginning balance**

5. **Total of all deposits**

6. **Total of all withdrawals**

7. **Ending balance**

8. **List of individual checks**

9. **Customer service telephone number**

10. **Account balancing section**

A checking account statement also includes the dollar **balance** at the beginning date, the total amount of deposits, the total amount of **withdrawals,** and the balance at the ending date. Finally, the statement lists each check paid by the bank since the previous month's statement. The back of most bank statements lists the steps needed to balance the account. Errors should be reported to the bank as soon as possible. The bank statement has the phone number and address needed to report an error.

The books of ancient Roman bankers were highly respected for their accuracy, especially with regard to dates. This allowed bankers' books to be used in courts of law as unshakable evidence.

Check entry in register

Deposit entry in register

Check listing on statement

In order to balance a checking account, compare your check register with the deposits and withdrawals listed on your bank statement.

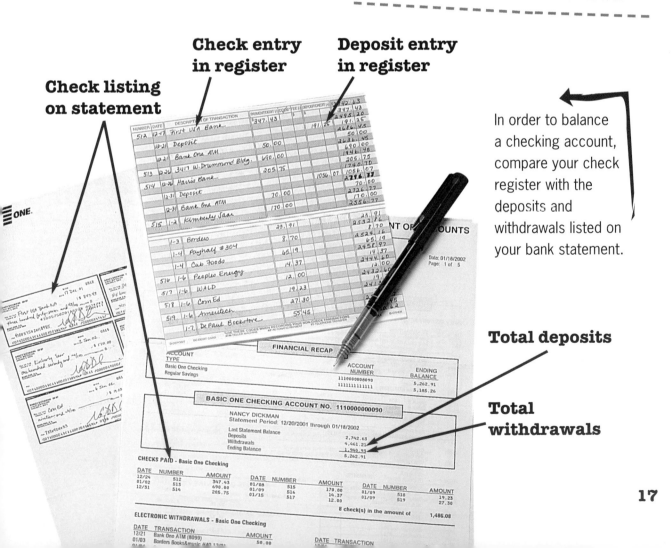

Total deposits

Total withdrawals

Processing Checks

Your bank processes checks written to you, and other banks process the checks you write. To do this, banks use a clearinghouse—an institution that allows banks to accept checks and make payments to one another using the smallest possible exchange of **funds**.

The key to processing checks is in the string of numbers printed along the bottom of a check. These numbers are printed with magnetic ink. Special machines called magnetic ink character recognition (MICR) devices can "read" the numbers. The information contained in the numbers is sent to a computer. MICR readers can process as many as 1,200 checks a minute.

THIS DOCUMENT MUST HAVE A COLORED BACKGROUND, ULTRAVIOLET FIBERS AND AN ARTIFICIAL WATERMARK ON THE BACK - VERIFY FOR AUTHENTICITY.

THE OAKWOOD SCHOOL
BUSINESS OFFICE
1101 MAGNOLIA BLVD. (818) 752-4400
NORTH HOLLYWOOD, CA 91601-3098

PAY

** Six hundred forty-eight and 00 / 100 Dollars **

TO THE
ORDER
OF

Bill Alain
9220 South Hi Point
Los Angeles, CA 90235-2601

BANK OF AMERICA
CENTURY CITY COMMERCIAL
2049 CENTURY PARK, EAST, SUITE 200
LOS ANGELES, CA 90067
16-66/1220

CHECK DATE	059035
	CHECK NO.
10/25/2001	
CHECK AMOUNT	59035
	$**648.00

VOID AFTER 90 DAYS

AUTHORIZED SIGNATURE

MP

⑆059035⑆ ⑆122000661⑆ 14177⑆06073⑆

The MICR numbers on a check identify the bank, the customer's account, and the check number. When the check is processed, its dollar amount is also added to the string of numbers.

MICR numbers

How a Clearinghouse Works

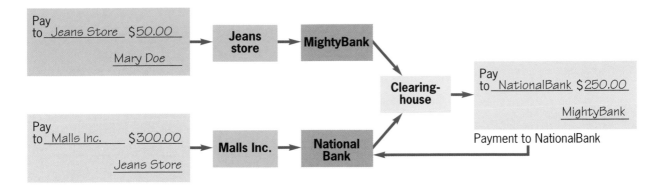

Here is an example of how a clearinghouse works. Suppose your checking account is at NationalBank and you write a check for $50 for new jeans. The jeans store **deposits** your $50 check in its account at MightyBank. At the same time, the jeans store sends a $300 check for store rental to Malls Inc. Malls Inc. deposits the $300 check in its account at NationalBank. Each bank sends the deposited checks to a clearinghouse.

The clearinghouse sorts and examines all the checks. It determines that NationalBank needs to pay $50 to MightyBank to cover your check, and MightyBank needs to pay $300 to NationalBank to cover the store's rent check. The payments can be made at the same time if MightyBank pays $250 to NationalBank.

By using a clearinghouse, the amount of money that needs to be **transferred** is as small as possible. This keeps things simpler for the banks. It also keeps the money safer—since less money has to be exchanged, there is less chance of it being lost or stolen in the process.

Paying Without Checks

Today, banks and consumers can **transfer** money without any cash or checks actually going anywhere. For example, monthly **Social Security benefits** can be **deposited** directly into an individual's checking or savings account. Many large companies deposit workers' paychecks directly into their personal accounts.

Many banks offer customers a way to pay for some **goods** and **services** automatically. A customer may use this option to pay bills such as a telephone bill or a car payment. The customer agrees to have the amount of the bill automatically transferred from his or her checking account to the telephone company's or car company's bank. Another way to transfer money without cash or checks uses a special telephone service.

Money in motion

Years ago, **transactions** requiring large amounts often required trainloads of money. At $30 an ounce—the price of gold in the 1930s—$1 million weighed more than 2,000 pounds (907 kilograms) and filled a large amount of space. To pay **debts,** tons of gold were physically moved from one location to another. As time passed, the trainloads of gold were replaced with suitcases of paper money. Today,

A standard gold bar is generally 7 in. (17.8 cm) x 3 5/8 in. (9.2 cm) x 1 3/4 in. (4.4 cm). It weighs approximately 25 pounds (11 kilograms).

banks and other **financial institutions** use Fedwire, a service offered by the **Federal** Reserve System, to safely transfer enormous amounts of money. In 2000, more than 100 million transfers were completed using Fedwire, averaging more than three million dollars each. These transfers are now able to occur without gold, paper money, or checks moving from one location to another.

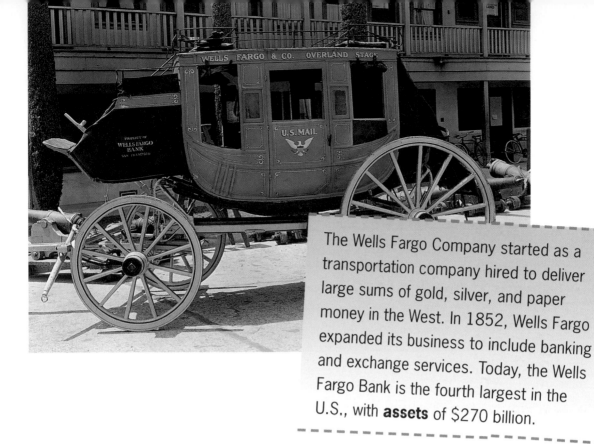

The Wells Fargo Company started as a transportation company hired to deliver large sums of gold, silver, and paper money in the West. In 1852, Wells Fargo expanded its business to include banking and exchange services. Today, the Wells Fargo Bank is the fourth largest in the U.S., with **assets** of $270 billion.

Some banks allow you to pay certain bills or to transfer **funds** from one account to another by telephone. You need to make arrangements with the bank before you can use this service.

Finally, many banks allow customers to complete different kinds of banking business using their personal computers. For example, customers may check their account **balances,** transfer money between accounts, or pay bills electronically. Banks use a special clearinghouse to process these electronic funds transfers.

Know It

A record of each automatic **withdrawal** should appear on your monthly bank statement. If the amount of the automatic withdrawal changes from month to month, you should be notified of the amount to be withdrawn at least ten days before the withdrawal takes place.

Charge Cards

In addition to cash and checks, people often use small plastic cards to pay for **goods** and **services**. These charge cards display the name of the company that **issued** them on the face of the card, along with the customer's name and account number.

A customer uses a charge card when checking out at a store. The card reader at the checkout line records the customer's personal information as well as the price of the purchase. The card reader sends this information to a computer at the company that issued the card. That company—American Express is one example—sends the customer a statement once a month. The statement includes a list of all the purchases the customer made in the past month, the cost of each, and the total cost of all purchases.

There is usually no dollar limit to the total amount of purchases a customer can make with a charge card. However, the customer must pay the entire **balance** each month. The customer pays a yearly fee to the card company for the use of the card. In addition, store owners who accept the card also pay a fee to the card company.

Charge it!

Charge cards, credit cards, and many kinds of identification cards have a black strip on one side. The strip is a thin ribbon of plastic. One side of the ribbon is coated with a magnetic material. The information the card carries is organized in a magnetic pattern on the ribbon.

A card reader is a little like the head of a tape cassette player. When the card is swiped through it, the reader recognizes the magnetic pattern and sends it over telephone lines to a computer. The computer matches the pattern with an account number assigned to a specific customer's name, address, and phone number.

As soon as it has identified the customer, the computer checks to make sure that the card is still valid and has not been reported stolen. It also checks to see that the dollar limit has not been reached and that payments are up to date. Then it sends a signal to the store telling whether the purchase is approved or not. This whole exchange may take only a few seconds!

Credit Cards

Like charge cards, credit cards can be used to make purchases at the checkout line. And as with charge cards, the credit card customer receives a monthly statement showing all the purchases made during the past month, the cost of each, and the total cost of all purchases.

Unlike with charge cards however, credit card customers do not have to pay the full amount due each month. No matter what **transactions** a credit card customer makes, he or she may choose to pay the full amount due or only a part of the full amount, as long as he or she makes at least the **minimum** payment listed on the monthly statement. The unpaid amount is carried over to the next month's statement.

Another difference between charge cards and credit cards is that credit cards have a dollar limit, called a credit limit. The total unpaid amount in any month must not be greater than the card's credit limit.

Customers paying credit card bills make payments to the companies that **issued** the credit cards, rather than the actual store where the purchases were made.

The first charge card used at a variety of locations was the Diners Club card, first offered in 1950. Before that, a charge card could be used only in the specific store that issued it, such as Sears or J.C. Penney. In 1959, Bank of America issued the BankAmericard. It was the first credit card to be accepted in stores and restaurants across the nation. BankAmericard eventually became the Visa card.

Credit talk

According to a recent study, two-thirds of college students have credit cards. One-fourth of these students got their first credit cards as high school students. Most people receive the first card they apply for. However, they do not usually investigate the meaning of the terms used by the credit card companies. Here is an overview of some of the more important terms.

Term	Definition
average daily balance	The amount found by adding each day's **balance** and then dividing that total by the number of days in a billing cycle. This is the method that most credit card companies use to calculate your payment due.
balance transfer	The process of moving an unpaid credit card **debt** from one card to another. Several balance **transfers** in a year may signal credit problems.
billing cycle	The number of days between the last credit card statement date and the current statement date.
cash advance fee	A charge for using credit cards to get cash. This fee may be a percent of the amount of cash received or it may be a flat fee. There is no grace period for a cash advance—**interest** is charged from the moment the money is **withdrawn**.
credit limit	The greatest amount a cardholder may charge on the card, also called a credit line. The Consumer Federation of America suggests people carry credit limits no greater than twenty percent of their total **income**.
grace period	The length of time you have to pay the credit card bill before you are charged interest on any new purchases. This applies only if you paid the previous month's balance in full.
introductory, or intro, rate	The low rate charged by a card company for an initial period to attract new cardholders, often called a teaser rate. After the introductory period is over, the rate increases.
penalty rate	An increased rate several percentage points higher than a card's current **annual** rate. **Penalty** rates may go into effect after two, or sometimes just one, late payments.
pre-approved	A "pre-approved" customer has passed a very basic credit-information screening. However, the customer's actual application may be turned down if the credit card company does not like the applicant's credit rating.

Credit Card Costs

Using a credit card can be costly. Most credit cards charge fees for a variety of reasons. For example, if a payment is late, there may be a late fee of $25 or $30. If the customer's unpaid **balance** is greater that the credit limit of the card, there may be a fee of $25 to $50. If a payment check is returned because there was not enough money in the customer's checking account, the customer may have to pay a fee of about $30.

A credit card's greatest cost is the finance charge—the **interest** charged on the unpaid amount. Interest is added to the unpaid balance of the bill every month. In this way, using a credit card is a bit like taking out a **loan** to pay for purchases made using the card.

Because of the way finance charges are calculated, it is best to pay a credit card bill as early as possible and to make the payment as large as possible. The only way to avoid the finance charge is to pay the full amount owed every month.

Know It

The 9 to 21 percent interest on a credit card is several times greater than the 3 to 5 percent interest banks pay for savings accounts. Credit card interest is also greater than the 3 to 9 percent interest charged for most new car loans and **mortgages.**

So many cards!

Credit card banking is the most profitable line of business for banks. In 1965, only five million credit cards were in circulation. Today, there are about 140 million credit cards in circulation in the U.S. Cardholders owe more than $500 billion, and they will charge $1 trillion this year.

Big fees

Some companies offer credit cards for people with bad credit or no credit. The application fees, **annual** fees, and interest rates for these cards are higher than for most other cards. Because these cards have high interest rates, it is best to pay the full amount due each month.

A customer's credit card billing statement gives a summary of activity on the account, including the balance, new purchases, past payments, credits, and finance charges. Important news about changes to the account is often included in a small-print flyer that is sent with the statement.

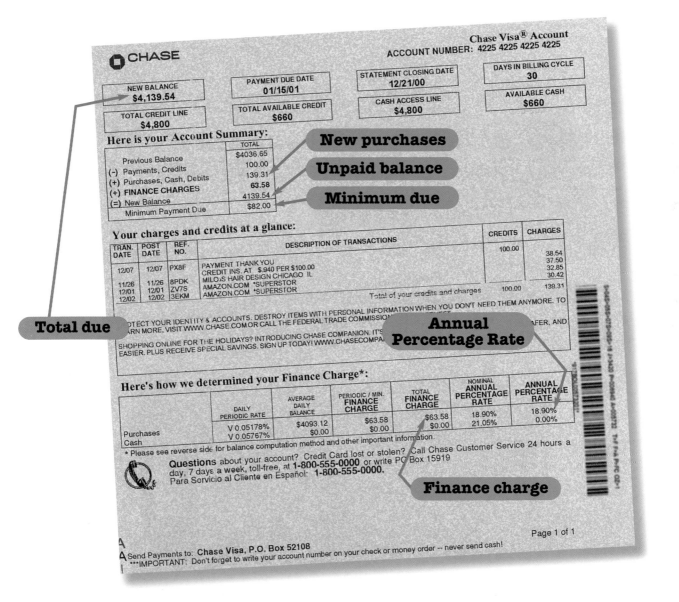

CHASE

Chase Visa® Account
ACCOUNT NUMBER: 4225 4225 4225 4225

NEW BALANCE $4,139.54	PAYMENT DUE DATE 01/15/01	STATEMENT CLOSING DATE 12/21/00	DAYS IN BILLING CYCLE 30
TOTAL CREDIT LINE $4,800	TOTAL AVAILABLE CREDIT $660	CASH ACCESS LINE $4,800	AVAILABLE CASH $660

Here is your Account Summary:

	TOTAL
Previous Balance	$4036.65
(-) Payments, Credits	100.00
(+) Purchases, Cash, Debits	139.31
(+) FINANCE CHARGES	63.58
(=) New Balance	4139.54
Minimum Payment Due	$82.00

New purchases
Unpaid balance
Minimum due

Your charges and credits at a glance:

TRAN. DATE	POST DATE	REF. NO.	DESCRIPTION OF TRANSACTIONS	CREDITS	CHARGES
				100.00	38.54
12/07	12/07	PX8F	PAYMENT THANK YOU		37.50
			CREDIT INS. AT $.940 PER $100.00		32.85
11/26	11/26	8PDK	MILO»S HAIR DESIGN CHICAGO IL		30.42
12/01	12/01	ZV7S	AMAZON.COM *SUPERSTOR		
12/02	12/02	3EKM	AMAZON.COM *SUPERSTOR		
			Total of your credits and charges	100.00	139.31

Total due

PROTECT YOUR IDENTITY & ACCOUNTS. DESTROY ITEMS WITH PERSONAL INFORMATION WHEN YOU DON'T NEED THEM ANYMORE. TO LEARN MORE, VISIT WWW.CHASE.COM OR CALL THE FEDERAL TRADE COMMISSION ... SAFER, AND SHOPPING ONLINE FOR THE HOLIDAYS? INTRODUCING CHASE COMPANION. IT'S ... EASIER. PLUS RECEIVE SPECIAL SAVINGS. SIGN UP TODAY! WWW.CHASECOMPA...

Annual Percentage Rate

Here's how we determined your Finance Charge*:

	DAILY PERIODIC RATE	AVERAGE DAILY BALANCE	PERIODIC / MIN. FINANCE CHARGE	TOTAL FINANCE CHARGE	NOMINAL ANNUAL PERCENTAGE RATE	ANNUAL PERCENTAGE RATE
Purchases	V 0.05178%	$4093.12	$63.58	$63.58	18.90%	18.90%
Cash	V 0.05767%	$0.00	$0.00	$0.00	21.05%	0.00%

* Please see reverse side for balance computation method and other important information.

Questions about your account? Credit Card lost or stolen? Call Chase Customer Service 24 hours a day, 7 days a week, toll-free, at **1-800-555-0000** or write PO Box 15919
Para Servicio al Cliente en Español: **1-800-555-0000**.

Finance charge

Page 1 of 1

A Send Payments to: **Chase Visa, P.O. Box 52108**
***IMPORTANT: Don't forget to write your account number on your check or money order -- never send cash!

4025

PAY TO THE ORDER OF

LIBERTY BANK

4025

The **interest** rate charged by a credit card affects the true cost of the card. Suppose you owe $3,000 on a credit card and you make no new purchases with the card. You may decide to pay $100 each month until the total **balance** is paid.

If the card has an interest rate of 9% a year, you will pay $411 in interest. If the card has a rate of 25% a year, you will pay $1,757 in interest—more than four times as much! It will also take you longer to pay off the balance at the higher rate.

Balance—$3,000
Monthly Payment—$100

Interest rate per year	Total Interest Paid	Number of Monthly Payments
25%	$1,757	48 (4 years)
23%	$1,507	46 (3 years, 10 months)
21%	$1,291	43 (3 years, 7 months)
19%	$1,102	42 (3 years, 6 months)
17%	$934	40 (3 years, 4 months)
15%	$784	38 (3 years, 2 months)
13%	$648	37 (3 years, 1 month)
11%	$524	36 (3 years)
9%	$411	35 (2 years, 11 months)

The amount of the monthly payment also affects the cost of the card. Again, suppose you owe $3,000 on a card and you do not charge any new purchases with the card. If the interest rate is 17% and you pay $100 each month, it will take three years and four months to pay off the bill.

However, if you pay only $50 a month at 17% interest, it will take eleven years and three months to pay the same bill. What's more, you will have paid $3,744 in interest alone—more than the original amount due!

Balance—$3,000
Monthly Payment—$50

Interest rate per year	Total Interest Paid	Number of Monthly Payments
19%	$6,534	191 (12 years, 11 months)
17%	$3,744	135 (11 years, 3 months)
15%	$2,580	112 (9 years, 4 months)
13%	$1,871	98 (8 years, 2 months)
11%	$1,376	88 (7 years, 4 months)
9%	$1,001	81 (6 years, 9 months)

Debit and Smart Cards

Today, computers and technology help to move information quickly from one place to another. This technology allows banks to offer debit cards to customers.

A debit card is used at checkout counters where the customer makes a purchase. The debit card acts like a check—the money for the purchase is **withdrawn** from the customer's savings or checking account and sent to the store's bank. It may take from two minutes to several days for the money to be **transferred** to the store's bank. The difference depends on the type of debit card used.

Online debit cards work like ATM **transactions.** They transfer **funds** immediately after the customer enters his or her personal identification number (PIN) into the store's card reader.

Debit logos

Some debit cards carry the MasterCard or Visa logo. These cards can be used at any place that displays the same logo.

Offline debit card transactions are a bit more like credit cards. The debit card is **swiped** and the customer signs a receipt. The system checks to see if the customer's account has enough funds to cover the purchase. The money is deducted from, or taken out of, the customer's account a few days following the purchase.

Know It

The magnetic strip on the back of a credit card holds a few dozen characters. Smart cards can hold thousands of characters.

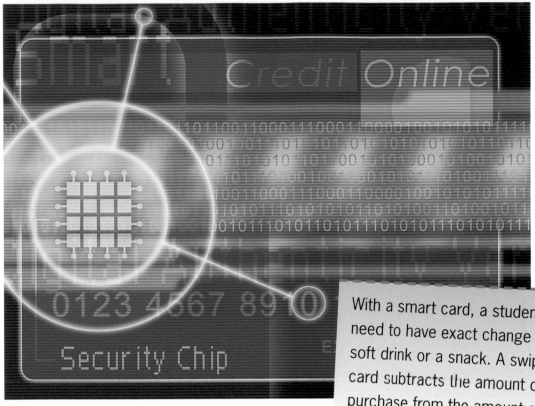

With a smart card, a student does not need to have exact change to buy a soft drink or a snack. A swipe of the card subtracts the amount of the purchase from the amount stored on the card.

The newest convenience for customers is a card called a smart card. This card is the size of a credit card, and carries a tiny computer chip pressed into its plastic. Special smart card readers allow the cards to do more than identify the customer and account.

One of the most common ways to use a smart card is to store money. When a customer wants to store a specific amount of money, he or she may pay in cash or have funds withdrawn from his or her account. This amount is then applied to the card. Each time the customer makes a purchase, the amount of the purchase is subtracted from the **balance** stored on the card, until all the stored value has been used.

If the customer uses all the money stored on the card, he or she can have the card "refilled," adding money to be stored on the card. One common example of a smart card is a phone card. It can be programmed with a specific amount of money to be used for telephone calls.

ATM Cards

The automated teller machine (ATM) is another **service** many banks offer. Using a special card and a personal identification number (PIN), customers can make **deposits, transfer funds** from one account to another, and **withdraw** limited amounts of cash. Banking customers can find ATMs at airports, grocery stores, sports stadiums, and many other places. Because most ATMs operate day and night, every day of the year, they make banking convenient for a bank's customers.

As with other banking services, ATMs often cost customers extra money. Some banks charge a fee ranging from one to three dollars for using an ATM. If a customer uses an ATM operated by a different bank, there may be a second ATM charge, also ranging from one to three dollars.

Know It

Customers must remember to note each ATM **transaction,** as well as any fees, in their checking or savings account records.

ATMs offer great convenience for a variety of bank customers. Most ATMs have Braille keypads to help customers who do not see well. Some ATMs are even programmed to talk to customers.

Never keep your personal identification number (PIN) in your wallet with your ATM card. If your wallet is lost or stolen, a thief will have the information needed to use the ATM to withdraw money from your account(s). Fortunately, having to remember a PIN may soon be a thing of the past. It is possible that soon some ATMs will identify customers by a pattern in their eyes. This pattern is as unique as fingerprints.

At the ATM

A person using an ATM makes choices at the ATM's terminal. The terminal is an input/output device that allows the customer to reach a computer in another place.

To use an ATM, a customer inserts a small card or **swipes** it through a card reader at the ATM terminal. The terminal screen asks the customer to type in a personal identification number (PIN) to make sure that the person using the card is its true owner.

Telephone lines connect the ATM terminal to a large computer. This computer keeps track of customer accounts and identification codes. The computer also determines what information will appear on the ATM screen. The information on the screen depends on what accounts the customer has and what transactions the customer wishes to make.

After the customer's business is finished, the ATM prints a receipt showing the type and amount of the transaction(s).

Loans

Loans are another kind of financial **service** offered by banks. A loan is an arrangement in which a lender, such as a bank, gives money to a **borrower.** In exchange, the borrower agrees to pay back the money, usually along with **interest,** at some future time. People use loans for a variety of reasons, such as to pay for education, buy a house, or start a business. Nearly all banks use the same loan application form. It asks for personal information and work history. It also asks about credit card **balances,** current car loans, and so on.

A law called the Truth in Lending Act requires that borrowers must be told the total cost of a loan before agreeing to it. They must receive, in writing, a clear record of the amount borrowed, the dollar amount of the interest charge, and the total amount to be repaid. In addition, the loan agreement must clearly show the interest rate in terms of the **annual** percentage rate, or APR.

This adult is co-signing for the teenager's loan. If the teen does not repay the loan, the bank will collect the money from the adult.

Amount of loan

Annual percentage rate

Amount of monthly payments

Total amount to be repaid

Loan fees

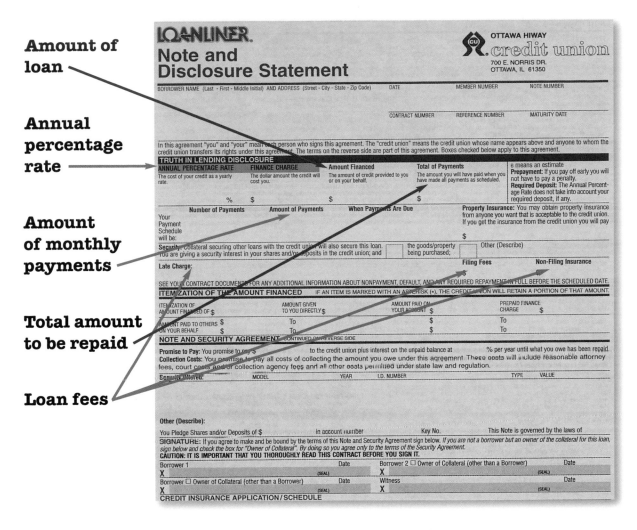

Sometimes a person may not meet all the requirements for taking out a loan. When this happens, the bank may require that the loan have a co-signer—a second person responsible for repaying the loan. The co-signer agrees to repay the loan if the borrower does not. The co-signer is also usually responsible for any fees, **penalties,** or other costs connected with the loan that the borrower does not pay. If a co-signer cannot or does not repay the loan, that fact becomes part of his or her own borrowing history. Information like this can cause the co-signer to be turned down later if he or she applies for a loan or other credit.

Because of **Islam's** restrictions on interest, Islamic banks make different arrangements with borrowers. For example, a borrower may pay a fee for a loan, or the bank may receive a share of the profits in a borrower's business.

Long-term Loans

The most common type of long-term **loan** is a **mortgage**, a loan to purchase real estate such as a house or farm. A mortgage usually requires regular payments for a specified period, often 15 or 30 years. If a **borrower** does not repay the mortgage as agreed, the bank that made the loan has the right to sell the home to get its money back. This process is known as foreclosure.

Mortgage loan officers consider several different kinds of information when reviewing mortgage loan applications. They compare a person's **income** to the probable housing expenses, including loan cost, property taxes, and insurance. In general, banks prefer that borrowers not spend more than one-third of their income on housing costs. That means a person earning $1,500 a month could pay up to about $500 for housing expenses.

Next, the loan officer compares the income to the regular expenses the person already pays. These include student loan payments, car loan payments, credit card **balances**, and child support payments. The applicant must have enough income to meet all these monthly payments as well as the mortgage.

People who lie about or misrepresent information on a mortgage application can be fined or even sent to prison.

Springfield Bank

Loan Application

Please Print in Ink

Application taken: ☐ in person ☐ by mail ☐ by telephone

Office # 141 Employee #

Employee Name **Amy J. Carr**

Date

APPLICANT INFORMATION

Name (Last) (First) (Middle Initial) Social Security Number

Address City State Zip Code How long at this address?

Do you own, rent or other? $ Monthly Payment Phone Number Purpose of Loan

Date of Birth $ Gross Monthly Income $ Other Monthly Income Employed Since

Employer Position

Note: Alimony, child support or separate maintenance income need not be revealed if Applicant or Joint Applicant does not choose to have it considered as a basis for repaying the loan.

Employer's Address Business Phone

Name of Your Bank Checking Account #

JOINT APPLICANT INFORMATION
(complete only if applying for joint credit with another person)

Loan officers also consider how the applicant has repaid car loans, credit card bills, and other expenses in the past. A bank may not grant a loan to people who have had several late or missed payments.

Employment, or work history, is important as well. Loan officers are more likely to lend money to people who have a steady work history, with several years at the same job or same type of work.

Mortgage rates

Shopping for the lowest mortgage **interest** rate is wise. For a 15-year mortgage, an interest rate of 7 percent saves more than $2,500 in interest compared to a rate of 7.5 percent.

15-year mortgage	7 percent	7.5 percent
Amount borrowed	$50,000.00	$50,000.00
Monthly payment	$449.41	$463.51
Total payments	$80,893.80	$83,431.80
Total interest paid	$30,893.80	$33,431.80

Longer-term mortgages cost more than those with shorter terms. During a 30-year mortgage, a homeowner will pay more than twice the interest paid during a 15-year mortgage at the same interest rate.

7 percent interest	15-year	30-year
Amount borrowed	$50,000.00	$50,000.00
Monthly payment	$449.41	$332.65
Total payments	$80,893.80	$119,754.00
Total interest paid	$30,893.80	$69,754.00

Short-term Loans

Some **loan** companies offer short-term loans, sometimes called cash advance loans or payday loans. The loans are usually for amounts from $100 to $400. To obtain the loan, an individual writes a check to the lender. The amount of the check is the amount of the loan plus a fee. For example, to borrow $100, an individual may write a check for $115. The lender usually agrees to "hold" the check as a promise of payment. In other words, the lender does not **deposit**, or cash, the check. In two weeks, the **borrower** pays the lender $115 in cash and the lender returns the uncashed check to the borrower.

The **transaction** seems easy and safe. However, most of the time the borrower cannot or does not pay the $115. Instead, he or she pays another $15 fee and the loan rolls over for another two weeks. After six weeks, the borrower will have paid $60 to borrow $100.

Short-term loans often have interest charges so great that the borrower has a very difficult time repaying the loan.

In some states, a cash advance or payday loan may have a legal **interest** rate as high as 871 percent! Twenty-three states and the District of Columbia have said that these lenders are not subject to laws preventing high-interest lending.

The Truth in Lending Act requires that—as with any loan—the cost of this kind of loan be disclosed. For this example, the **annual** percentage rate, or APR, is 390 percent! That means a $100 loan, taken for one year, would cost $390 in interest. There are some states that limit the amount of interest lenders can charge, but even those limits are high. A borrower would be smart to look for other ways to get the money needed before agreeing to take out one of these loans.

> ## Know It
> Do not confuse the terms **debt** and debit. A debt is a loan or **mortgage** owed to another person. A debit is a bookkeeping entry of something owed.

Other options

Because of the finance charges associated with payday loans, it would be wise to consider any and all other ways of dealing with a money problem. After all, paying 390 percent APR is truly a bad deal.

- If you need credit, shop around. Look for credit with the lowest APR. You might consider a small loan from your credit union or a small loan company. Perhaps your employer would be willing to give you an advance on your pay. There may be a family member or close friend willing to lend you the money.

- Check into using a credit card to borrow money with a cash advance. Find out the terms, fees, and interest rate.

- Ask your **creditors** for more time to pay your bills. The electric and gas companies may be willing to accept partial payment for a month or two. Perhaps your landlord will accept a late rent payment, along with a late fee.

- Call any credit card companies to whom you owe money. Tell them your situation and ask what arrangements they can offer. Be sure to find out the cost for this **service.** Will there be a late charge? An additional finance charge? Will they increase the interest rate?

If you decide you must use a payday loan, borrow only as much as you can afford to pay with your next paycheck and still have enough to make it to the next payday.

Establishing Credit

When a person applies for a **loan**, the bank usually wants to know about that person's credit—the way he or she handles money matters, and his or her ability and intention to pay.

The Equal Credit Opportunity Act (ECOA) ensures that all people have an equal chance to get a loan. This does not mean that every person who applies for a loan will get it. It does mean that a person applying for a loan should be judged fairly on his or her **income**, expenses, **debt**, and credit history. The credit history of a person is an important part of deciding whether or not to grant a loan.

Know It

Although they do not advertise the service, some community banks offer Visa and MasterCards. Sometimes the **interest** rate for these cards will be less than the rates charged by large, national credit card corporations.

This couple is applying for their first credit card. They want to establish credit so that they will be able to get a **mortgage** in the future.

40

There are several ways to establish a credit history. For example, a new customer can get a credit card **issued** at a local or community bank. The bank may require that the customer also open a savings account at the bank. If the customer agrees to leave his or her money in the account for a year, the bank will then issue a credit card. Usually, the person will not be allowed to use the card to spend more than the amount on **deposit.** If the customer pays the bills from the credit card on time, he or she will have established a good credit history.

A bank's customer service department can help a customer who wants to establish credit. Some banks allow a customer to open a savings account for a certain amount, such as $1,000, for a specified time. The bank allows no **withdrawals** during that time. Meanwhile, the bank lends $1,000 to the customer, arranging for repayment in twelve monthly payments. Once the loan is repaid, the customer can withdraw money from the savings account. The history of repaying the loan establishes the customer's credit.

Meet the Mae Family

Because higher education is important but expensive, the government sponsors corporations to help grant and oversee student loans. These include Sallie Mae (Student Loan Marketing Association) and Nellie Mae (Nellie Mae Education Foundation). There are also government-sponsored corporations who work to make sure that mortgage **funds** are available for low- and middle-income people. Fannie Mae (Federal National Mortgage Association), Ginnie Mae (Government National Mortgage Association), and Farmer Mac (Federal Agricultural Mortgage Corporation) work in a variety of ways to make mortgage money available. However, they do not grant mortgages directly.

Credit Reports

When a bank is considering granting a **loan** to a person, it checks the person's credit history before deciding. First, the bank reviews the information on the loan application. Next, the bank reviews the person's credit history reported by a credit bureau or a credit reporting agency. These businesses keep track of people's credit histories.

Banks, credit card companies, and other lenders give credit bureaus information about how individuals pay their bills. With this information, a bureau starts a file on each individual. In addition to the information sent by banks, credit bureaus get public record information from courthouses around the country. A person's public record lists legal information about that person. For example, public records show an individual's marriages and divorces. This kind of information goes into the person's credit history file as well.

Know It

Although every lender has different guidelines, as a general rule, people should have no more than five or six open credit card accounts—major cards and department store cards combined—to be in good standing. It is very important that all payments be made on time.

Home buying tied to credit

Few people seem to be aware of how important their credit rating is to getting a home **mortgage.** The length of your credit history and your payment record together account for half of your credit score. A less than acceptable rating may mean lenders will not grant a mortgage, or will offer one with higher **interest** and substantial fees.

Today's college students seem to be among the least aware. Nearly one in four students owes more than $3,000; one in ten owes more than $7,000. They build this **debt** at a time when they have little or no **income** to pay it off.

Experts suggest that credit cards be used only for emergencies—real emergencies. One parent's description of emergencies may be helpful: If you can eat it, drink it, or wear it, it's not an emergency.

Credit bureaus do not approve or reject loan applications, but simply report information. It is up to the lender—the bank, credit card company, or other **financial institution**—to decide whether or not to grant a loan. Loans can be denied based on income, length of residence, or employment history, in addition to credit history.

There are three major credit reporting agencies in the United States: Experian, Equifax, and Trans Union. These and other agencies keep credit histories of more than 170 million Americans and provide more than a half billion credit reports a year.

A credit report includes a person's name, age, address, and **Social Security** number. There is information on home, car, or school loans and credit cards: the amount paid last, the highest amount charged, and whether payments were on time or late.

Fixing Credit Problems

Sometimes people have problems with their credit. Late or missed payments may mean that a person owes more than he or she can pay. A poor credit report may stop a company from offering a car **loan** or prevent a bank from granting a **mortgage**. In addition, a poor credit report can make it harder to get or keep a job. Some employers use a credit report when they hire and evaluate employees for promotion. By law, an employer must get your permission to look at your credit report.

There are organizations that specialize in helping individuals with their credit problems. Most of the organizations call themselves credit counseling services. They are usually **nonprofit,** and work with a person to solve his or her credit problems for free or for a small fee. Some will work with **creditors** to reduce **interest** rates and monthly payments. They may even get some creditors to drop interest charges altogether. However, not all creditors participate in such programs.

A **consolidation** program for repayment may help some people. In this kind of program, an individual makes a single monthly payment to the consolidation company. The company uses that payment to make all the monthly payments the individual owes.

Know It

A sure sign of credit problems is using one credit card to make the payment due on a second credit card. Anyone in this situation should seek help from a credit counseling service.

Negative information can remain on a credit report for seven years. After seven years, the credit reporting agency is required by law to remove the negative entries from the credit file. The exception is bankruptcy, when a person can no longer pay their **debts** and the court divides their property among their creditors. That information stays on file for ten years.

Changing your ways

You can change a poor credit rating if you take charge of it, replacing poor credit habits with wise spending practices.

- Use credit only for needs, not wants.

- Don't charge anything you can't pay cash for or can't pay off in 30 days.

- Read the information on credit card and loan applications carefully to avoid expensive terms or conditions. The fine print often contains rules that might charge you costly **penalties.**

- Write due dates on calendars. If you are fewer than 30 days late, you will not be reported to a credit bureau as late. However, if your payment arrives after the due date, you will owe a substantial late fee.

- Pay more than the **minimum** due on your credit card **balance.**

- Work with a nonprofit educational service to make a **budget** you will be able to follow.

The individual agrees to make regular and timely payments until the debt is paid off. The plan might take four years or longer to complete, and its interest charges may be high. However, at the end of the repayment period, all the debts will be paid.

Fix Credit Problems:

CreditCounseling is a not-for-profit agency dedicated to helping consumers who are seriously behind in their payments. We have twenty years' experience in working with creditors and consumers. We take pride in restoring our clients' credit health.

(202) 555-1234

This type of advertisement can be found in your phone book or local newspaper.

Check your report

The Federal Trade Commission estimates that 47 percent of Americans have errors in their credit reports. Over half of those errors are great enough to lead a lender to deny a loan.

Open a Savings Account

Start to learn how to use the **services** of a bank in your area today. Choose a nearby bank. You might find a small community bank more inviting than a large nationwide bank.

Find out what you need to open a savings account at the bank. How much money will you need to open an account? Will you need someone over eighteen to open the account with you? Be sure to ask how much **interest** the savings account will earn.

If you have a savings account passbook, keep it in a safe place. Add a few dollars to your savings account at least once a month. You might want to make your **deposit** equal to the price of a movie, a CD, or a concert ticket.

At the end of the year, notice how much money is in the account. Compare that amount to the amount of money in the account at the beginning. Keep on adding to the account.

Glossary

annual occurring or done every year

asset total value of a company

balance amount of money in an account

benefit something that happens or is given for the good of a person; advantage

borrower person who takes or receives something, like money, with the promise of returning it

budget plan for handling money, including earnings and expenses

consolidation group of things combined into one, such as debts

creditor person or business to whom money is owed

debt something that is owed

deposit to put in, as money into a bank account, or the amount put in

economy use or management of money

federal describing a union of states that share a government

financial institution company that deals with the management of money

funds money

good thing that can be bought and sold

grant gift of money for a specific purpose

income money received for work or from other sources

interest amount charged for the right to use or borrow money

Islam religion that follows Allah as the one god and Muhammad as his prophet. Believers of Islam are called Muslims.

issued given out or distributed

loan money given to a person with the understanding that it will be paid back with interest

merchant person who buys goods in one place and sells them in another, often a different country

minimum least possible amount

mortgage money given to a person to buy a house or other piece of real estate with the understanding that it will be paid back with interest

nonprofit not set up to make a profit

penalty punishment for breaking a rule; in banking, usually involves paying a fee

salary set amount of money paid for work over a certain period of time

service work done for another or others

Social Security government program of retirement benefits

swipe to slide with a sweeping movement

transaction act of conducting business

transfer to move from one place to another

unearned income money received without doing any work for it

wage payment for work based on the number of hours worked or the rate of production

withdraw to remove, such as money from a bank account

More Books to Read

Macht, Norman. *Money and Banking*. Broomall, Penn.: Chelsea House, 2001.

Simpson, Carolyn. *Choosing a Career in Banking and Finance*. New York: Rosen Publishing Group, 1999.

Sobczak, Joan. *Banking*. Vero Beach, Fla.: Rourke Press, Incorporated, 1997.

Index